Each a Piece

by Bruce Brooks

illustrated by Elena Pavlov

A Laura Geringer Book

An Imprint of HarperCollins*Publishers*

A piece of the moon

a part of the sky

two words
from a tune

a dog passing by

a ball that was thrown

by a hand far away

the sunlight
that shone

long ago in the day

the shape of some blocks

that fell in a heap

the stretch
of a yawn

that leads

on to sleep—

Each piece
is a part

of more left to find

and whatever's
missing—

is all in your mind.

To Cole

with all my love

—E.P.

Each a Piece   Text copyright © 1998 by Bruce Brooks   Illustrations copyright © 1998 by Elena Pavlov   Printed in China.   All rights reserved.   http://www.harperchildrens.com
Library of Congress Cataloging-in-Publication Data   Brooks, Bruce.   Each a piece / by Bruce Brooks ; illustrated by Elena Pavlov.   p.   cm.
"A Laura Geringer book."   Summary: Rhyming text and illustrations with some cut-outs reveal that things are often more than they seem at first.   ISBN 0-06-023594-2   1. Toy and
movable books—Specimens.   2. Toy and movable books.   [1. Visual perception—Fiction.   2. Stories in rhyme.]   I. Pavlov, Elena, ill.   II. Title.   PZ8.3.B787Eac   1998   93-45951
[E]—dc20   CIP   AC   Typography by Tom Starace   1 2 3 4 5 6 7 8 9 10   ❖   First Edition

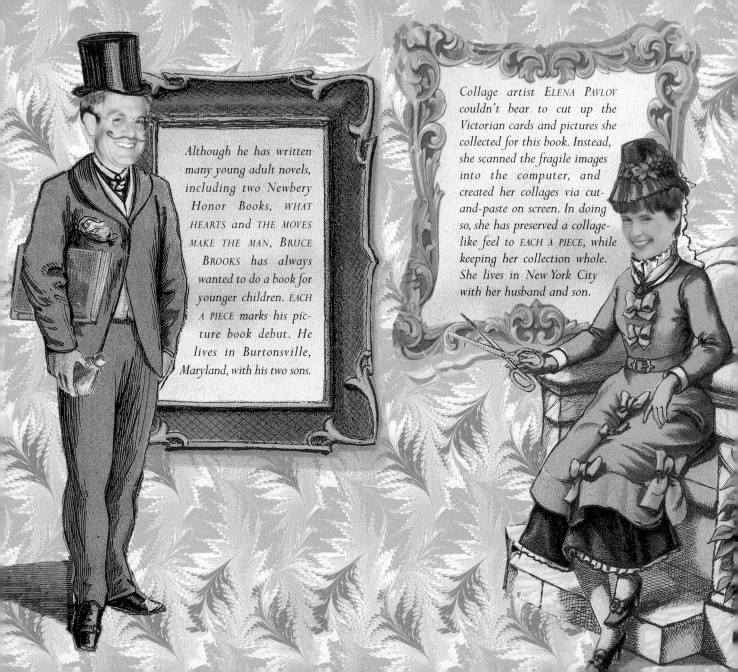

Although he has written many young adult novels, including two Newbery Honor Books, WHAT HEARTS and THE MOVES MAKE THE MAN, BRUCE BROOKS has always wanted to do a book for younger children. EACH A PIECE marks his picture book debut. He lives in Burtonsville, Maryland, with his two sons.

Collage artist ELENA PAVLOV couldn't bear to cut up the Victorian cards and pictures she collected for this book. Instead, she scanned the fragile images into the computer, and created her collages via cut-and-paste on screen. In doing so, she has preserved a collage-like feel to EACH A PIECE, while keeping her collection whole. She lives in New York City with her husband and son.